Advice To A Young Man Upon First Going To Oxford

by

Edward Berens

Advice To A Young Man Upon First Going To Oxford
by Edward Berens

ISBN: 978-93-59958-32-3

Published by

DOUBLE 9 BOOKS

2/13-B, Ansari Road
Daryaganj, New Delhi – 110002
info@double9books.com
www.double9books.com
Tel. 011-40042856

ABOUT THE AUTHOR

Edward Berens, an insightful and articulate creator, pens the incredible work "Advice to a Young Man upon First Going to Oxford." In this compelling e book, Berens affords worthwhile recommend and steerage to younger guys embarking on their academic journey at Oxford University. His writing displays a deep expertise of the demanding situations, experiences, and possibilities that watch for those college students as they step into the esteemed organization. With a blend of wisdom and practicality, Berens imparts advice on navigating the instructional, social, and private facets of university existence. His phrases resonate with a sense of mentorship, imparting perspectives that now not handiest help in the educational pursuit however also in fostering non-public growth and man or woman improvement. Berens' paintings stands as a testament to his dedication to shaping and nurturing the minds of younger students, equipping them with the tools needed to thrive in their collegiate endeavors. "Advice to a Young Man upon First Going to Oxford" is a comprehensive and insightful guide, reflective of Berens' ardour for schooling and his desire to support and prepare the adolescents for the demanding situations and possibilities that lie beforehand of their educational adventure at one of the world's maximum prestigious educational establishments.

CONTENTS

LETTER I
SENSE OF RELIGION

MY DEAR NEPHEW,

It gives me sincere pleasure to hear that you have actually become a member of the University of Oxford. This satisfaction, perhaps, may in some degree be attributed to the pleasing recollection of my own Oxford life, but certainly it arises principally from anticipation of the substantial benefits which you, I trust, will derive from your connexion with that seat of learning. At the same time, I will own that my satisfaction is not entirely unmixed with something like apprehension. An University education has many and great advantages, but it also is attended with many temptations;—temptations to which too many young men have yielded, sometimes to the great injury of their character, and the utter ruin of all their future prospects.

In fact, you are now entering upon the most important period—the *turning point*—of your whole life. You have become, in a great measure, your own master. For though you will be under a certain degree of discipline and *surveillance,* yet in a multiplicity of cases you will have to act for yourself—to take your own line. You will have to contend against the allure ments of pleasure and dissipation, and you have just reached the age when the natural passions and appetites become most impatient of restraint. At the same time, you will be exposed to the influence both of the example and of the solicitations of lively young men, who will try to carry you along with them in their career of thoughtlessness and folly, and who will think it strange, and *show* you that they think it strange, if you run not with them to the same excess of riot. Against all these moral trials and temptations, your best safeguard will be found in a strong sense of religion, kept habitually present to your mind. You must endeavour, according to the language of Scripture—(and in writing to you I shall always gladly make use of the very words of Scripture, when they suit my purpose, as having a force and an authority which no other words can possess)—you must endeavour to *set the Lord always before you*. Never for a moment forget that you are continually in the presence of that awful Being, who can, and who will, call you to a strict account for all that you do amiss. Nothing can excuse your forgetting Him.

If you at all believe in a Supreme Being, the Creator and Governor of the world; if you believe that God is, and that he is a rewarder of them that diligently seek him, and at the same time an avenger to execute wrath upon every soul that doeth evil, the least particle of common sense or common feeling will tell you, that nothing should be put in competition with his will. When his will is clear, it *must* be obeyed without hesitation. I am sure that you will assent to this. If religion is any thing, it is *every thing*. It is, indeed, the one thing needful, in comparison with which every thing else sinks into insignificance, into nothingness.

Endeavour, then, to keep up in your mind and heart this habitual sense of religion by every means in your power. It will require from you considerable care and attention. The lively spirits natural to your time of life, and the thoughtless levity of some of the young men into whose society you will be thrown, will have a tendency to make you think less of religion, if not to induce you entirely to forget it. Be ever on your guard against thus swerving from your allegiance to your Creator.

Nothing will contribute more to preserve you from this danger than regularity and earnestness in your private devotions. When you rise in the morning, seek from God spiritual strength to enable you to resist and overcome the temptations to which you may be exposed during the day. Every night implore his forgiveness for your many failings and transgressions, and his protection against the dangers which surround you. Suffer nothing to induce you to neglect private prayer.

You will of course be required every day to attend chapel. Consider such attendance not as an irksome duty, not as a mere matter of routine and college discipline, but try to regard it as a privilege, and to take a real interest and pleasure in it. Acquire the habit of joining fervently in the prayers, and of constantly deriving from the lessons and other portions of

Scripture, the doctrinal and practical instruction which they were intended to convey. Many college chapels are furnished with Greek Testaments and Septuagints. You will judge from experience, whether following the lessons in the Greek assists in fixing your attention, or whether it diverts it from the matter to the language. My own opinion is in favour of the practice.

Make a point of giving to Sunday as much of a religious character as you can. I am not recommending a Jewish strictness. Let Sunday be a day of cheerfulness; but let your reading and your thoughts, as far as may be, partake of the sacred character of the day.

The study of the Scriptures constitutes an important part of your preparation for your degree. This study will furnish an appropriate employment for a considerable portion of the Sunday. Always attend the University Sermons. I recommend this not merely as a branch of academical discipline, but as a means of religious and intellectual improvement. The sermon will generally, I believe, be worth attending to. The select preachers are chosen, for the most part, from the ablest men in the University; men, several of whom are likely hereafter to fill the highest stations in the Church. You will seldom be driven to have recourse to the advice of the pious Nicole in his Essay, *"des moyens de profiter de mauvais sermons."* The various modes in which different preachers enforce or illustrate the same great truths, and the diversities of their style and manner, may afford you matter—not of ill-natured criticism—but of useful reflection. Some colleges require their under-graduates to give every week in writing a summary of the sermon which they have heard at St. Mary's. If you adopt this practice, you will find it contribute greatly to fix your attention, and to give you a habit of arranging and expressing your ideas with facility and readiness. Of course, some preachers deserve this steadiness of attention much more than others.

It is, I trust, unnecessary to remind you of the duty of receiving the Lord's Supper, whenever it is administered in your college chapel. In some colleges, nearly all the under-graduates partake of this ordinance; in others, I believe, almost all neglect it: at least this was the case formerly. In such and similar cases, you must be guided, not by common practice, not by the example of numbers, but by what you know to be your duty. If you feel any doubt or difficulty, frankly mention it to your tutor. There are, I am persuaded, few tutors now in Oxford, who would not be able and willing to assist you with their advice.

This attention to your religious duties need not be attended by any preciseness or austerity of manner. On the contrary, I should wish you to be at all times cheerful and good humoured, ready to take part in any innocent gaiety. My object is to impress upon you the absolute necessity of always putting religion in the *first place*. If you really believe what you profess to believe, do not hesitate as to shewing it in your conduct. Never be so weak as to be ashamed of doing what you know to be your duty. Never be guilty of such unmanly cowardice as to be ashamed of avowing your allegiance to your Creator and your Redeemer.

I remain,
My dear Nephew,
Your affectionate Uncle.

LETTER II
CHOICE OF FRIENDS, AND BEHAVIOUR IN SOCIETY

MY DEAR NEPHEW,

Among the many advantages of an University, few rank higher, both in general estimation and in reality, than the opportunity which it affords of forming valuable and lasting friendships. Indeed this advantage can hardly be rated too highly. I look back to the intimacies which I contracted at college, as among the greatest blessings of a life, which has been eminently blessed in various ways. I still hold intercourse with many of my Oxford friends, whose characters and attainments do honour to the place where their education and their minds were matured. And even the recollection of most of those, who have been removed from this lower world, is attended with a soothing melancholy, which partakes more of pleasure and thankfulness for having enjoyed their society, than of pain. *The memory of the just is blessed* 14:1 .

I hope, my dear nephew, that you will improve this advantage to the utmost. In your intimacies, however, endeavour to be guided rather by judgment than by mere fancy. Sameness of pursuits, similarity of dispositions and inclinations generally contribute much to throw men together; but be careful not to attach yourself to any man as a *friend*, unless he is a man of moral worth, and of real religious principle. Intimacy with a man who is unrestrained by religion, *must* be attended with great danger. Your own natural appetites will continually solicit you to forbidden indulgences, and will not be kept in due subjection without difficulty. If their solicitations are seconded by the example and by the conversations of an intimate associate, your peril will be extreme. Intimacy with a man of bad principles and immoral character, may utterly blast all your prospects of happiness both in this world and the next.

You will of course have the greater power of *selection*, if your general acquaintance is pretty extensive. I acknowledge, that my opinion is rather in favour of your forming an extensive acquaintance, provided that you never suffer it to encroach upon your time, or to lead you into any compromise of religious principle. Going to the University constitutes a sort of entrance into the world, an introduction to manly life; but this advantage is lost if you seclude yourself altogether from society. In order, however, to acquire or to retain such an acquaintance, your manners and general demeanour must be acceptable or popular.

One of the first requisites, in order to be thus acceptable, is the neglect, the forgetfulness of *self*—a readiness to put *self* in the back-ground. Any obtrusion of self, any appearance of self-love, self-interest, self-conceit, or self-applause, tends to expose a man to dislike, perhaps to contempt.

One way in which this disregard, this abandonment of self, must show itself, is real unaffected humility. Most of the external forms and modes of modern politeness, its bows and obeisances, its professions of respect and service, its adulations, are nothing but an affectation of such humility, and bear witness to its value when it exists in reality. When it does so exist, and still is free from any servility of manner, any unworthy compliances, nothing contributes more to make a man acceptable and popular in society. It inflicts no unnecessary wounds on any one's pride or self-love. And, you will observe, that it is the temper and behaviour, inculcated by the general spirit and by the particular precepts of religion, which bids us *in honour to prefer one another*; and says, *in lowliness of mind let each esteem others better than himself.*

Another requisite is, a willingness to please and to be pleased. Some men seem to think it beneath them, and a mark of littleness of mind, to wish or to try to please any body, and wrap themselves up in a cold superciliousness. Others seem determined never to be pleased with any thing or any person, but are always finding fault. They have no eye for, no perception of, merits or beauties, either external or internal, but are keen and quick-sighted in detecting blemishes, and eloquent in exaggerating them20:1 . If any person's good qualities, or any work of art or of genius is commended, they are sure to throw in some observations calculated to depreciate and disparage them. And with respect even to the works of Nature, and the dispensations of Providence, they are more ready to see and to point out evils, than to acknowledge advantages. This temper—this habit of disparagement— is certainly very unamiable; and justly offensive, not only to those who are run down by it as its immediate objects, but to all who witness it. A man who consults his own comfort, or the comfort of those with whom he associates, should be disposed to make the best of every thing. I would by no means wish him in the slightest degree to compromise truth, or to make the remotest approach to flattery; but I would have him see every thing in the most favourable point of view, and disposed to pursue and to dwell upon what is good rather than upon what is bad. Too much of that which is bad is sure to be forced upon our attention, without our taking any pains to look out for it.

Be always on your guard against hurting the feelings, or even shocking the prejudices, of those with whom you associate. A little observation, and some attention to your own feelings in similar circumstances, will soon teach you what is likely to be annoying to others. Make every allowance for their self-love, and for attachment to their own opinions.

Never give unnecessary pain or mortification. It is *unnecessary*, when it can be avoided without compromising the consistency of your own character, or hazarding the interests of religion and of truth.

In short, my dear nephew, if you will study St. Paul's account of the nature and properties of charity, and regulate your temper and your behaviour accordingly, you will want little in order to be a perfect gentleman, in the highest sense of the word. I will not enter upon this account in detail, but must refer you to Fenelon's excellent book on this subject, if it should come in your way, or even to my own Sermon22:1 . Give me your attention, however, for a minute or two, to a few slight remarks upon charity—merely as it bears upon our conduct in society.

Charity suffereth long—μακροθυμει—it bears patiently with other men's defects of temper, discourteousness of behaviour, and awkwardness of manner; and is *kind*, gentle, and obliging—χρηστευεται.

Charity envieth not—ου ζηλοι. It is free from those little jealousies, and rivalries, and emulations, which, where they are admitted, sometimes give sourness to the temper, and bitterness to the behaviour.

Charity *vaunteth not itself*—ου περευεται; it is not rash or over hasty; it is not overbearing, positive, and peremptory, in language or manner; *is not puffed up*—ου φυσιουται; is not inflated with an opinion of its own worth or consequence; and, that being the case, it doth not behave itself unseemly—ουκ ασχημονει; it does not treat other men with disdain and superciliousness.

Charity *seeketh not her own*—ου ζητει τα ἑαυτης—that is, she is not *selfish*. Charity neglects not altogether her own concerns, or her own interests, but does not attend to them exclusively; does not *so* attend to them, as to be unmindful of, or inattentive to, the interests and welfare of others.

Charity is not easily provoked—ου παροξυνεται. Nothing more disturbs the peace and comfort of society than the being easily provoked. When a man is touchy and waspish, he is always looking out for, and catching at, occasions of offence.

Charity rejoiceth not in iniquity, but rejoiceth in the truth; it does not take pleasure in hearing of misdoings and evil conduct, but delights in accounts of praiseworthy actions, and in the spread of sound religious principles.

Charity *beareth all things, believeth all things, hopeth all things, endureth all things*; παντα στεγει, παντα πιστευει, παντα ελπιζει, παντα υπομενει.

I will not, my dear nephew, lengthen a long letter, by endeavouring to point out the precise meaning of these expressions. You may understand from them, that charity is patient of ill-usage; that instead of being suspicious and disposed to cavil and carp at every thing, it is open and ingenuous, ready to give men credit for speaking the truth, when there is no good reason to think otherwise; and that it is disposed to hope the best, to think as favourably as it can of those with whom it comes in contact; and if it cannot actually think well of them at present, to *hope* for their amendment and reformation.

I think you will agree with me, that a man influenced by this spirit would be an acceptable man in society, and that the best practical Christian would be the best gentleman[26:1] .

I remain,
Your affectionate Uncle.

14:1 Prov. x. 7.
20:1 See Numbers 72, 74, and 98, of the Rambler.
22:1 See Village Sermons.
26:1 See Jones's Letters from a Tutor to his Pupils.

LETTER III
CONVERSATION

MY DEAR NEPHEW,

I take it for granted, that upon first going from school to Oxford, and entering into society different, in many respects, from any that you have hitherto been accustomed to, you feel some of that shyness which belongs to the character of most Englishmen. I should be sorry if you did not. You probably feel diffident, too, of your ability to bear your part in general conversation, and an apprehension of being, on that account, set down as a stupid fellow. But don't be uneasy. More young men, I am persuaded, hurt themselves by talking too much, than by talking too little. When a fresh-man, at first starting, is quite at his ease, and talks readily upon any subject that happens to be uppermost, some of his companions may be amused at his coolness, but most of them will be disgusted. If, by your look and manner, you show that you are alive to what is said by others, and now and then throw in a remark, not destitute of meaning, you will be more generally popular than one of those random talkers. Men of a certain standing, qualified by their liveliness or by their information to bear a leading part in conversation, do not like to see an undue share of it engrossed by others, especially by a mere youngster. They greatly prefer a good listener to a ready talker.

Young practitioners in Doctors' Commons have, I believe, to pass through their year of silence, before they are allowed to speak. During the period of silence, they quietly observe, and become acquainted with, the usages and practice of the court. Something similar to this period of quiet observation, might not be inexpedient for a noviciate in society. At all events, never talk for talking's sake; never speak unless you have something to say worth attending to.

You will, I am sure, my dear nephew, take it in good part, if I point out a few of the conversational faults, of which young men are apt to be guilty. It is natural that we should talk most of that in which we are most interested. Now, of all things in the world, a young man feels most interested in *himself*. But if, in consequence of such feeling, he ventures to talk much of himself, of his own habits, his own pursuits, his own feelings, his own achievements, he will very soon be set down as a bore and a conceited coxcomb. A young man naturally feels a strong interest, an interest increased by separation, in his own immediate family. This feeling, with some young men, is so deep, that they shun the mention of any thing closely connected with their *home* as a sort of profanation, a desecration of things sacred. With others, this feeling takes the opposite direction, and leads them—*celebrare domestica facta*—to introduce the concerns of their own nearest relations into the conversation of a mixed party. Take care that you never are guilty of such a violation of good taste and correct judgment. Interesting as your home and its inmates are to *you*, nothing can well be less interesting to those, who are unacquainted with them. It will be a stretch of courtesy and good-nature, if they tolerate the mention of them without some expression either of ridicule or of distaste. If you speak of your home-concerns at all, let it be only to one or two intimate friends, who, from the regard which they feel for *you*, may be supposed to take an interest in all belonging to you.

Be on your guard against getting into the habit of telling long stories: they generally are tiresome. Many circumstances, in addition to the feeling that you have them to tell, may give them a consequence in your eyes, which they do not in reality possess. Lively anecdotes, or short narratives, told with spirit, are among the most amusing ingredients in conversation; but even with them, if you often meet the same company, there is considerable danger of falling into repetition.

Never be guilty of falling into the too common practice of indulging in scandal, the practice of talking of men disparagingly, of running down their character behind their backs. I by no means wish you to flatter any man, whether present or absent, or to speak favourably of character or of conduct which does not deserve it. But beware of *detraction*. Nothing is more unamiable in any man, especially in a *young* man; and, what is of infinitely more consequence, nothing is more opposite to the spirit and the precepts of religion, which repeatedly enjoins us to *speak evil of no man*. Bear in mind the advice of one of the most sagacious and penetrating observers of human nature:—*Whether it be to a friend or foe, talk not of other men's lives; and if thou   canst, without offence, reveal them not* 34:1 . *If thou canst without offence;*—circumstances may require that the truth should be revealed,—that the real truth should be spoken and made known, even though it should be injurious,—though it should be absolutely fatal to another man's character. But do not take pleasure in telling any thing to another's prejudice; do not make the tearing of a character in pieces a matter of amusement. By such conduct you would not only be guilty of a gross violation of Christian charity, but will probably bring yourself into many scrapes in a worldly point of view. In a mixed company, there may chance to be some friend or connexion of him, whom you are running down; or, at all events, what you say will be repeated,—*a bird of the air will carry the matter*,—till it comes to the ears of the injured person. And what will be the consequence? A feeling of aversion and dislike, a spirit of hostility to you, will, not unnaturally, be engendered, both in him and in such of his friends and connections as are acquainted with the circumstance.

One of the most unwarrantable kinds or forms of detraction, is the attributing of any man's conduct to corrupt or unworthy motives. A man's real motives are known only to God and to himself; indeed, very often to God *alone*, as from the deceitfulness and intricacy of the human heart, a man himself is sometimes ignorant as to what his real motives actually are. Certainly it is rash and presumptuous for any other man to pretend to decide upon them, and most uncharitable and unjust to pronounce them to be corrupt, when they are capable of a favourable interpretation. Express your disapprobation of unworthy actions as strongly as you please; but beware of rash and uncharitable censure, and especially beware of the presumption of imputing to any corrupt and evil motives.

As I have cautioned you against violating Christian charity in conversation, so I must warn you against infringing on Christian purity. You have arrived at a period of life, when your utmost care and vigilance will be requisite, to keep your natural passions and appetites within proper bounds. Indeed, all your care will be ineffectual unless assisted by Divine grace. Do not take part in conversation which is calculated to add to their importunity or to their strength. Thoughtless young men, under the influence of these feelings, sometimes indulge in *foolish talking and jesting* 37:1 , of most pernicious tendency, and most inconsistent with the Christian character. Avoid and discourage conversation of this nature, so far as you possibly can. Do not add fuel to a flame which already burns but too fiercely. *Fools make a mock at sin* 38:1 ; and none but *fools* should be capable of making a joke of temptations and vices, which in themselves are awfully serious, which lead on to eternal ruin.

I hope you will never be so unfortunate, as to fall much into the company of men, who make a jest of religion, or of any thing connected with religion. Those who are bent upon following the guidance of their own appetites, and their own wills, naturally dislike that which would check and restrain them. They are consequently apt to become *scoffers*, and to attempt to turn religion and its sanctions into ridicule. Avoid the society and conversation of such men, as you would avoid the plague. If unhappily thrown among them, discountenance them to the utmost.

Do not indulge yourself in a habit of raillery or banter. Raillery is a difficult thing to manage well, and very apt both to give pain to him who is the object of it, and to reflect discredit on him who attempts it. Sometimes you see one or two young men, of more liveliness than sense, picking out some quiet person in company as a *butt*, at which they may point their wit, and carrying on an attack of banter and ridicule. This is, probably, not only annoying to him, but tiresome and painful to all the right feeling men who chance to be present.

I am glad to join in, or to witness, a honest hearty laugh, when any thing really calls for it. Beware, however, of the practice of laughing when there is nothing to laugh at. Some people fall into a way of giving the accompaniment of a laugh to almost every thing that they utter, especially if they have any direct intention to be jocular. This habit is disagreeable to most of those who witness it. It proceeds, I believe, generally from a sort of shyness and awkwardness contracted in early youth, and is, as I know from experience, difficult to get rid of. It certainly is inconsistent with the manners and habits of good society. Be always the last to laugh at your own jokes, or your own *good* stories. If they are really worth laughing at, the company will find it out, and by premature or excessive laughter you will mar their effect.

As you get on in society, you will probably often fall into discussion and argument. When this is the case, take care not to be too positive or peremptory in your manner. Be solicitous to allow their full weight to the arguments of your antagonist. Do not suffer the impression of the force and correctness of your own reasoning, to render you blind to what is urged against you. Above all, keep your temper. If you lose your temper, victory will be deprived of its credit, and defeat will be more disgraceful. At the same time you will run a double chance of being defeated, without having the wit to see, or the manliness to own it. Believe me, my dear nephew, (to adopt the very words of one of the most sagacious and distinguished of modern statesmen) "that the arms with which the ill dispositions of the world are to be combated, and the qualities by which it is to be reconciled to us, and we reconciled to it, are moderation, gentleness, a little indulgence to others, and a great deal of distrust of ourselves; which are not qualities of a mean spirit, as some may possibly think them, but virtues of a great and noble kind, and such as dignify our nature as much as they contribute to our repose and fortune; for nothing can be so unworthy of a well-composed soul, as to pass away life in bickerings and litigations, in snarling and scuffling with every one about us. Again and again, my dear,—we must be at peace with our species; if not for their sakes, yet very much for our own43:1 ."

But my letter grows long, and I must hasten to conclude it. Read repeatedly Cowper's lively poem on conversation, which seems to me to have much of the spirit and accurate moral taste of Horace, with the elevation derived from Christianity. Read, too, if you can lay your hand on it, Bishop Horne's paper on conversation, in the Olla Podrida. In these two essays you will find many of the sentiments which I have expressed, only given in a much more engaging manner. In the 78th and 83d Numbers of the Idler, many common faults in conversation are exposed with a degree of humour, in which our great moralist did not very frequently indulge.

I remain,
My dear Nephew,
Your affectionate Uncle.

34:1 Ecclus. xix. 8.
37:1 Ephes. v. 4. and Coloss. iii. 8.
38:1 Prov. xiv. 9.
43:1 Prior's Life of Burke, p. 215. Second edition.

LETTER IV
AGAINST YIELDING TO THE INFLUENCE OF NUMBERS

My dear Nephew,

When I advised you to fall in, so far as you reasonably can, with the wishes and inclinations of those with whom you associate, you understood, I trust, that compliance should never go so far, as to involve the slightest sacrifice of truth or of principle. When carried to this culpable extent, it becomes an instance of weak and unmanly cowardice.

One of the greatest dangers to which young men are exposed upon their first entrance into the world, is that which arises from their readiness to be swayed by the example or by the persuasion of their companions. The example, and still more the persuasion, of a single individual, is sometimes not without difficulty resisted, and the difficulty of resistance is greatly increased by the influence of numbers. A young man dreads the imputation of singularity. He cannot bear to stand out against the example, perhaps the solicitations, of those among whom he lives. He suffers himself, therefore, to be carried along by the stream, and led into conduct, of which, in his conscience, he utterly disapproves.

Never, my dear nephew, do you be guilty of such weakness. Avoid singularity, whenever it can be avoided with innocence: an affectation of singularity for singularity's sake, generally proceeds from conceit or self-sufficiency. But where the path of duty is clear, let no example or persuasion induce you to swerve from it. Keep ever impressed upon your mind the admonition of Scripture, *Thou shalt not follow a multitude to do evil.*

Never suffer yourself to be laughed out of what is right. Never be ashamed of adhering to what you know to be your duty. In matters of duty keep in mind the words of Scripture, *Fear ye not the reproach of men, neither be afraid of their revilings.* Never expose yourself to the censure justly cast upon those who value the praise or the approbation of men,—of giddy, thoughtless, sensual men, more than the praise of God. Remember, my dear nephew, the solemn warning of our Lord: *If any man shall be ashamed of me and of my words in this adulterous and sinful generation, of him shall the Son of man be ashamed when he cometh in his glory with his holy angels.*

In your steady adherence to the dictates of conscience, you will always find some who will respect you for it; or, even if you should stand alone, like Abdiel, "among the faithless, the only faithful," you will be supported by the testimony of your own heart, and by an humble confidence in the approbation of the Almighty. One or two instances may, probably, make my meaning more clear.

Perhaps a few joyous spirits have devised some scheme of irregular, sensual gratification,—of Bacchanalian revelry;—or, perhaps, two or three dunces, whose intellects and moral feelings are of such a stamp, as to render them rather impracticable subjects for academical discipline, have contrived some plan of impotent resistance to the college authorities, or some plot of petty and vexatious annoyance, in order to give vent to their mortification, when such silly resistance has been proved to be ineffectual. Wishing for the screen or protection of numbers, they will try to persuade their companions, that they will be wanting in manly spirit, or in social feeling, if they refuse to join them. And is there, after all, any thing so very *spirited*, any thing of high-minded and noble daring in behaviour, which seeks to screen itself by concealment and subterfuge, and which, if detected, braves, not any personal danger or suffering, but merely the terrors of an imposition? If the offence is so aggravated as to entail the heavier penalty, rustication, or expulsion, such punishment inflicts, indeed, severe grief upon the parents and friends of the offender; but he himself, with the short-sightedness of folly, perhaps almost enjoys the idleness and the freedom from academical restraint, to which rustication consigns him. A young Oxonian is apt to feel very indignant if not treated by deans and tutors, as a man and as a gentleman; but has he any right to expect to be so treated, if he condescends to adopt the practices of a mischievous or a truant school boy?

I am no friend to the unnecessary imposition of oaths; but, I own, I do not see how any thing like deliberate and systematic opposition to academical authority, can be reconciled with the oath of academical obedience taken by every freshman. I know well that the usual construction of that oath,—(I doubt not the legitimate construction)—is, that the person who takes it will obey the statutes, or submit to the penalty imposed upon the infraction of them. I am aware, too, that the violation of the strict letter of many of the statutes is acquiesced in, and almost sanctioned, by those in authority; but surely a *deliberate* and *contumacious* contravention of the statutes, accompanied by a natural endeavour to evade punishment, is hardly consistent with the spirit of the oath. Certainly it is inconsistent with the spirit of Christianity, which everywhere inculcates a dutiful submission to the constituted authorities; a compliance, in all things lawful, with the regulations of the place in which we are, and of the society which has received us among its members. No man is compelled to go to the University; but if he does go thither, he should make up his mind to comply with its rules, during the short period of his residence.

Perhaps, my dear nephew, you may think that I have all this time been combating, or, rather, seeking to *lay*, a phantom of my own raising; that I have been making mole-hills into mountains; or, like Don Quixote, turning wind-mills into giants: but, in my long Oxford life, I have heard of so many instances of the silly behaviour of which I have been speaking, that I wish to put you on your guard against it. True manliness consists in adhering to what you think to be right. In keeping steadily to the path of duty, notwithstanding the solicitations, or the taunts, or the ridicule of your associates, there is more proper spirit and moral courage, than in braving the rebuke or the impositions of a dean or a proctor.

I remain,
My dear Nephew,
Your affectionate Uncle.

LETTER V
IMPROVEMENT OF TIME

MY DEAR NEPHEW,

I trust that you are now hard at work. I can figure you with your Herodotus before you, your Scapula on one side, and your maps on the other, *setting-to* in good earnest. You have, I am sure, fully determined to make the most of your time. The time which you must necessarily pass in Oxford, in order to take your bachelor's degree, is but little after all. Your whole actual residence, during the three years, will probably not much exceed a year and a half. Certainly, of this *modicum* of time you cannot afford to waste any portion. Make a point of devoting it to real study, to real strenuous exertion. You owe this to yourself—to your own credit and character; you owe it to your parents, who have probably put themselves to some pecuniary inconvenience, in order to give you the advantage of an Oxford education; you owe it to God, to whom you are responsible for the employment of your time, as well as for the proper use of your other talents. Fix in your mind and memory the lesson taught you by the sun-dial in the Quadrangle at All Souls—"*Pereunt et imputantur;*" or that of another similar monitor—"*Ab hoc momento pendet æternitas.*" Take time for exercise; take time for relaxation; but make steady reading your object and your business. Do not be so weak, or so unmanly, or so vain, as to be ashamed of being known to read. You went to Oxford on purpose to study; why should you be ashamed of keeping that purpose in view?

In the choice of your studies, be guided implicitly by the advice of your tutor. Very likely you may not see the use of some branches of science, or of reading some particular books. But do not fancy that in such matters you are wiser than older men, who have maturely considered these things again and again. If you mean to be your own guide and your own teacher, you had better have staid away from Oxford altogether. It is one great advantage of academical education, that a definite course of reading is marked out for you. When a young man,—indeed, when *any* man,—is left entirely to his own choice, he is apt to be distracted by the many different branches of study, the many different books, which present themselves, and to fall into a habit of desultory reading, productive of little lasting benefit. You are saved from this distraction and perplexity, throw ing upon other shoulders the trouble and responsibility of making a proper choice.

I believe almost every tutor now in Oxford, will direct his pupils to devote a certain portion of their time to the highest of all studies—the study of religion. Some knowledge of religion is absolutely indispensable, in order to pass your examination for your degree. But independently of all academical objects, you cannot help feeling satisfied that time so employed, is employed well and wisely. Such study, with the blessing of God upon it, will be beneficial to you through the whole of your future existence, both in this world and the next.

Among the many advantages of an university education, must be reckoned the opportunity of attending public lectures, such lectures especially, as are illustrated, by an expensive philosophical apparatus, or by the inspection of actual specimens. The experiments conducted by means of such apparatus, and the handing round of specimens, are not only absolutely essential, oftentimes, to the comprehension of the science to which they belong, but contribute powerfully to fix it in the memory. If you can spare the time from your severer studies, and if your tutor does not disapprove, I should strongly advise you to attend in succession the lectures on natural philosophy,—on chemistry,—on mineralogy,—and on geology. Some acquaintance with these sciences, is in itself so interesting and useful, and is now so general, that you ought not, I think, to miss your present opportunity of acquiring it: so favourable an opportunity you will hardly meet with again.

Much may be done by a judicious distribution of your time. When you have made such a distribution, keep to it steadily. Be peremptory with yourself in adhering to it, and be peremptory in preventing others from encroaching upon it,—from encroaching upon it, at least, unnecessarily. I suppose that, upon the average, you may get four or five hours' steady reading before dinner, and three or four after. This will leave you abundant time for exercise, for relaxation, and for society. Certainly it will not spare you any for mere *lounging*; either for lounging yourself, or being lounged upon by others. If you cannot avoid the latter by any other means, you will be reduced to the alternative of shutting your door, or, if that term is still in use, of *sporting oak* against them. If they reproach you, set them, as their punishment, to read the paper in the Idler on the robbery of time[62:1] .

Either of your time, or of your money, waste as little as possible upon newspapers. I admit, that of all periods of history, the time in which we actually live is, *to us*, the most interesting. I admit that, both with a view to your taking part in the conversation of general society, as well as upon other accounts, some knowledge of passing events is desirable, or even necessary. For such purposes, a rapid glance at the newspaper, or even what is picked up by hearsay, will, generally speaking, be sufficient. While reading for your degree, however, you really cannot spare time to read the newspapers *through*. The most important portions of them are, perhaps, the debates during the session of parliament, and the trials. Of the debates, a considerable part is very trifling and unprofitable; and, in order to read with real advantage those speeches which are most deserving of attention, it is necessary to be possessed of a considerable portion of that knowledge of history, of legislation, of political economy, of mercantile and financial transactions, the *foundations* of which you are at Oxford engaged in laying. It is not to be wished that an under-graduate should affect to be an experienced politician, prepared to give a strong and decided opinion upon subjects, upon which able and experienced men, possessed of ten times his knowledge, find a difficulty in making up their mind. In the reports of trials, many curious facts, and much interesting information are to be found. In order to understand many of them, however, it is requisite to have a more intimate acquaintance with the rules of English jurisprudence, and with the practice of the courts, than can be expected in a young man as yet hardly set free from the eggshell of school. Upon the subject of newspapers, however, I will say no more. I well know, that in merely touching upon it, I tread upon delicate and debateable ground.

Take sufficient time for relaxation; but let your relaxations, as far as you can, be intellectual and improving.

Oxford now presents opportunities, both of acquiring some knowledge of natural history, and of cultivating a taste in the fine arts, which it by no means possessed when I was an under-graduate. For these we are principally indebted to those two admirable brothers[66:1] , who have so long devoted their time, their money, their distinguished talents, and their various attainments, in the first place, to plans of beneficence, and in the next, to the advancement of science and the cultivation of taste. It is to them that we owe the enlargement, the arrangement, and in fact the greater part of the contents, of the Museum, which now contains a very interesting collection of specimens, particularly in British ornithology. To them we are indebted for the excellent casts (in the Radcliffe Library) from the most perfect specimens of sculpture, and for the beautiful models (in the Picture Gallery) of the most celebrated remains of ancient architecture. The Picture Gallery itself contains many paintings, which, if not of any great excellence as works of art, yet are well deserving of attention on very many accounts; and the copies from the Cartoons, especially if you can be assisted with a few hints from Richardson or Sir Joshua Reynolds, are most interesting objects of study and contemplation. I am surprised that the young men in Oxford make so little use of these advantages. Many of them seem hardly to be aware of their existence.

Among other modes of relaxation, not unconnected with intellectual improvement, I should advise you to make yourself a little acquainted with our early English architecture. If you can buy or borrow either Bentham's Essay on Gothic Architecture, or Milner's accurate and elegant Treatise on the Ecclesiastical Architecture of England during the middle ages, you will need no other assistance, excepting, indeed, a friend disposed to go along with you in this pursuit. Oxford and its immediate neighbourhood will furnish you with many interesting specimens from the Saxon and Norman, in the cathedral, St. Peter's in the East, and Iffley church, down to the utter depravation of the art, or rather the total change of style, in the time of Henry the Eighth.

These interesting pursuits, however, I mention, as you must follow them, if you follow them at all, merely *by the by*. They must not be suffered to interfere with your severer studies. When engaged in those studies, give them your whole undivided attention. *Whatsoever your hand, or your head, findeth to do, do it with all your might.*

The habits of study and of intellectual improvement, which you acquire at Oxford, you should carry with you into the vacation. During the vacation, you may, perhaps, take more time for society — the society especially of your own immediate family — and more for relaxation; but still do not *waste* your time; still consider yourself as responsible for the right employment of it. Make sure of the ground which you gained during the term, by going over by yourself, what you then read with your tutor. Improve your acquaintance with the standard writers of our own country, and acquire some knowledge of modern history. In short, make the most of your leisure. Read Bishop Home's sermon on redeeming the time, and the papers in the Spectator and the Rambler to which he refers. Read, *and learn by heart*, what is said on the loss of time in the second of Young's Night Thoughts:

> "Part with it as with money, sparing; pay
> No moment but in purchase of its worth."

But my letter grows long, and (you will say) tedious.

I remain,
My dear Nephew,
Your affectionate Uncle.

62:1 Vol. I. No. 14.
66:1 John Duncan, Esq. and Philip Duncan, Esq. of New College.

LETTER VI
PUNCTUALITY

MY DEAR NEPHEW,

I ventured to give you some advice respecting the employment of your time; perhaps I ought to follow up that letter with a few remarks upon punctuality. Unless you acquire the habit of punctuality, you will be apt, not only to lose your own time, but to make unjustifiable inroads upon the time of other persons.

Endeavour, therefore, to *keep to your time* in every appointment, whether the appointment be made by yourself or by others, (the college authorities for instance,) whether it be with a superior, an equal, or an inferior. Whether it be in a matter of business or in a matter of pleasure, try always to be true to it. Let this be your system and your habit. Some deviations from punctuality may now and then be unavoidable; but do not let them occur unless they *really are* unavoidable in fairness and reason. If you have yourself made an appointment, your word is, to a certain degree, pledged to your keeping to it. The case is in some measure the same, when, though the appointment is actually made by others, you have acceded to it.

Want of punctuality seems to proceed either from pride and superciliousness, or from some infirmity, some weakness of character. Most men try to be punctual in any appointment with a man of rank superior to themselves, especially if they have any object, any interest, in conciliating his favour. And, on the other hand, too many persons seem to feel themselves at liberty to be unpunctual in an appointment with an inferior. It is not worth while, they think, to care about being exact with one so much beneath them. "Let him wait till I am at leisure to attend to him," exclaims such a man, in the proud consciousness of superiority; and, perhaps, some trifle, or mere indolence, is all that he has to plead for his neglect.

You, my dear nephew, have, I trust, long since learned, that you have no right to treat any man, however low his rank may be, with disrespect, — with any thing approaching to contempt. You well know, that both reason and religion require us to regard all men as our brothers, and that one of the golden rules of the latter is, *in lowliness of mind, let each esteem others better than himself.* Whatever a man's rank in life may be, he has a right to punctuality as he has a right to truth; and you have no right, by your unpunctuality, to rob him either of his time or his patience. Certainly you have no right to give him by such means the painful feeling that he is neglected, and neglected because he is despised.

And thus, also, with men of your own age and your own rank in life; in all the little engagements and appointments, whether of business or of pleasure, which occur in the common intercourse of society, endeavour still to maintain the habit of punctuality. As every man wishes to have the character of being true to his word, so it will be to your credit to have the character of being true to your engagements, whether those engagements relate to great matters or to small.

But though want of punctuality is sometimes occasioned by pride, it must more frequently proceed from a certain degree of weakness of character, or from mere indolence. A man acknowledges punctuality to be right and desirable, but cannot muster up sufficient energy and resolution. He cannot prevail upon himself to quit his bed, or his easy chair, or his fire-side, or the employment by which he chances to be occupied, till the time fixed on has passed away. His friends are kept waiting; those who have business to transact with him lose their temper; they, again, are perhaps disappointing others, and all because he had not sufficient decision of character, sufficient command of himself, to be punctual.

You may remember seeing at my house my friend Mr. M.78:1 He was at Oxford a very good-humoured fellow, and every body liked him; but he never could contrive to be in time for any thing. He got imposition upon imposition for being too late for chapel; he came to dine in hall when other men were going away; and his friends were almost afraid of making an appointment with him, either for business or for amusement, because they knew beforehand that he would not keep it. When, after leaving Oxford, he established himself as a country gentleman in his paternal mansion, the same habit still clung to him. No time was fixed for any thing, or if it was fixed, it was never kept. Neither his guests nor his servants knew at what hour either breakfast, or dinner, or any other domestic arrangement, would take place. Consequently, their time and their spirits were wasted in uncertainty. When engaged to dine at a neighbour's, perhaps he would forget the engagement altogether; or, if he chanced to remember it, would not arrive till the master of the feast had given him up in despair, after allowing possibly an extra half hour, during which, the solemn pause which sometimes takes place before dinner, had become more solemn, from the annoyance of seeing a whole party kept waiting by the unpunctuality of one person. The servants, meanwhile, were yawning and fidgetting backwards and forwards in the listlessness of expectation; the cook perplexed with the sore dilemma of seeing all the productions of her skill, either chilled with cold from being kept back, or burnt to a cinder; and the temper even of the lady of the house a little out of tune, from the certainty that the dinner would be spoiled. Of all these various vexations, the sole cause was to be found in Mr. M.'s want of energy. He could not bring himself, perhaps, either to shorten a pleasant ride, or to lay down a book which interested him, or to quit his own chair by the fire-side, in order to dress. The convenience and comfort, and for a time the good humour, of a whole company, were to be sacrificed to his indolence, his *vis inertiæ*, and unpunctuality.

Never permit yourself, my dear nephew, thus to trifle with the time or the temper of any persons, whether high or low, with whom you have any intercourse. Make a point of always being in time. I think it is said of Lord Nelson (though I cannot hit upon the passage in his life), that when some friend was fixing an appointment of importance at a certain hour, the hero added, "Say a quarter *before*—to that quarter *before*, I have owed all my success in life." I do not advise you actually to be *before* the time of an engagement, which some people will complain of as being worse than being too late, but be so much beforehand as to be master of your time, or to have it in your power to be punctual almost to a minute. When you are received as a guest in a friend's house, consider compliance with the hours and habits of the family, as a natural return for the hospitality which is shown to you. There is something incongruous in seeing a young person deranging, by his unpunctuality, the economy and regularity of a whole household. And do not suffer the kindness and indulgence of your parents to induce you, when with them, to be less attentive to punctuality than you are, when with other persons of superior age or rank to yourself. Never let them wait for you; make a point of being always ready. An excellent friend of mine lays it down as a maxim, that *habitual unpunctuality is positive incivility.*

I have alluded to the unpunctuality of one of my college friends: I will contrast it with the punctuality of another. The latter when at Oxford was distinguished for lively talents, and for an exuberance of spirits bursting forth into every possible variety of fun. He is now the owner of a spacious and splendid mansion, with a large establishment of servants, and often a considerable number of guests, attracted by his many amiable and excellent qualities. He still retains his playfulness of wit, but his domestic arrangements are a model of punctuality. Family prayers, and every meal, are to a minute. His guests and servants, consequently, know exactly what they have to depend on, the arrangements of the day, whether for business or for amusement, can be made with precision, and every thing is done at its proper time. This is punctuality on a greater scale. You and I, my dear nephew, must attend to it in smaller matters.

I remain,
My dear Nephew,
Your affectionate Uncle.

78:1 Mr. M. is imaginary.

LETTER VII
AMUSEMENTS

MY DEAR NEPHEW,

In a former letter I recommended to you certain modes of relaxation, having some connection with intellectual improvement. You will, perhaps, tell me that you want relaxation more entire and complete; that the intellect requires perfect rest; that you must have *amusement* in the strict etymological sense of the word. You may be right. I have already advised you to take sufficient time for *exercise*, and the exercise of the body will generally give rest and refreshment to the mind.

In your choice of amusement, however—amusement, I mean, as combined with exercise—you must have strict regard to economy, both of money and of time. Do not think me an old woman, if I add, that regard for *both* should keep you from any excessive bodily exertion, such as will unfit you for study, or seriously affect your health. I am told that the latter effect has of late, not unfrequently, been the result of over fatigue in *rowing*; that many young men have died at an early age; that others live on with all their powers debilitated, from having overstrained their nerves, and their whole muscular system, in boat-races. Rowing is in itself a salutary and delightful species of exercise; and the facility of practising it, is one among the many advantages of Oxford; but when carried to the excess which I have alluded to, it is foolish and culpable.

I would have a young man regardless of danger, willing to risk limbs, health, or life itself, for the benefit of his fellow-creatures. He should, like Hamlet, "hold his life at a pin's fee," when any adequate object is to be answered by putting it in jeopardy. But a man has *no right* to risk either his life or his limbs for a bravado, in mere idle vanity and ostentation. Such wanton risk is cruelty to his parents and friends, and a presumptuous tempting of Providence.

Riding, for riding's sake, must, with your finances, be out of the question. The utmost that you ought to allow yourself, is a hack once or twice a term, for some specific purpose—to visit a distant friend, perhaps, or to see some interesting object lying beyond the range of a walk. What I have said of riding, applies, with ten-fold force, to hunting, which entails expense—(the hire of a hunter, the hire of a hack probably to take you to cover, sundry ostlers and helpers, and very likely a jovial dinner at an inn)—utterly inconsistent with an average allowance; which entails, also, a waste of time, which, in the short period of an Oxford residence, can ill be spared.

What shall I say of *cricket*? I have great respect for cricket, as a national and a manly game. The demand which it makes upon your Oxford time is confined to the short term between Easter and the long vacation, and it does not require a very large portion of the day. It is not *necessarily* attended with any expense. Whether the incidental expenses of *uniform* (if you belong to a club), tent, dinner, &c. &c. are such as you can fairly afford, is for your consideration. They need not be high, and, in my good will to the game, I am anxious that they should be kept down.

Tennis is an animated game, of much variety in itself, and requiring great variety of muscular exertion. It is connected with many historical and chivalrous recollections, and carries the mind back to our Henry the Fifth and the "mocking Dauphin" of France. As it cannot be played without a spacious and expensive edifice, it is altogether an aristocratic game, and demands an aristocratic purse. It is a game which requires a good deal of practice, and, consequently, a good deal of expenditure, in order to acquire a tolerable degree of skill; and your skill will seldom have an opportunity of showing itself after you have quitted Oxford, as you will seldom fall in with a tennis-court. I have no hesitation in saying, that you, my dear nephew, have no money that you have a right to spend upon yourself in this manner.

You will never, I trust, annoy any of the neighbouring country gentlemen, by attacking their game. You know how tender a point this is, and how susceptible most landed proprietors are upon the subject; and your own good feeling, and sense of propriety, and common fairness, will prevent you from trespassing in this manner. You can imagine how indignant you would yourself feel at such an invasion, and will not be guilty towards another of a wrong, of which you would complain loudly if it were offered to yourself.

After all, *walking* is the cheapest exercise, and, perhaps, the best. If you wish to give it variety, you will find plenty of ditches to leap, steeps to ascend, and hills to run up or down. And, dull as are most of the great roads leading into Oxford, the country round abounds in interesting objects within reach of a walk. There is much natural scenery, possessed of a good deal of variety and picturesque character; and there are many buildings, and remains of buildings, which either from something in themselves, or from adventitious circumstances, well deserve to be looked at. The church at Cumnor, for instance, not only has within itself much to interest a man fond of architectural or antiquarian investigation, but, in common with the remains or site of Cumnor hall, and the village of Dry Sandford, have acquired a sort of classical notoriety from the magical pen of Sir Walter Scott. The picturesque ruins of the kitchen, and other buildings at Stanton Harcourt, the slight vestiges of Godston Nunnery, the Town Hall, the Gaol, and the two churches at Abingdon, may all become, each in its turn, the object of a pedestrian expedition. The residence of the Speaker, Lenthall, at Bessilsleigh, may deserve notice, from historical recollections, though for no other reason. The Saxon church in Iffley I have already mentioned. The recently-built Saxon chapel at Kennington is done in excellent taste, and is a most gratifying instance of the munificence and piety of an individual clergyman, devoting, I believe, almost all his resources to the work. The church at Wytham will show you that a church very lately erected may, by correct judgment, be made to present the appearance of having been built five hundred years ago. But I must not go on in this way, or you will think that you have got hold of an Oxford guide. Most of the villages and village churches in the neighbourhood, have some character of their own worth examining.

So much for amusements connected with exercise, which has led me into something like a repetition of some of the sentiments in a former letter.

A few words on sedentary amusements.

If you read *in earnest*, and are bent upon making the most of your time, you will have little of it left for amusements of a sedentary nature.

The less you have to do with cards the better. Young men can have no occasion for the assistance of cards in order to pass their time; and there seems to be something almost incongruous in the idea of *their* sitting down to a rubber. Nor do they need the excitement: if they wish for it, that very wish is a reason why they ought not to have it. If they play for money — or, at all events, if they play for such sums as make the winning or losing an object of any degree of consequence — they become gamblers; and of the many bad passions which gambling sometimes calls into activity, and of the destructive consequences which it entails, no one is ignorant. If you once get into the habit of playing, you will, perhaps, not know when to stop. Cards are very seductive, and you may find yourself become a gambler almost before you are aware of it. Perhaps the best plan is *not to know* how to play, which furnishes an answer always ready.

Chess is a game of elegance and interest, and the being a good chess-player, carries with it a certain impression of general ability and of intellectual activity and resource. Perhaps I may allow that playing at chess adds a certain degree of interest to the perusal of the history of a campaign, whether ancient or modern, with its various moves, its checks and counter-checks, its retreats and *castlings*. But chess is a fascinating game, and will be apt to make larger demands upon your time than you can afford. If you indulge in it at all, you must be peremptory with yourself in resisting its tendency to incroach either upon your time or your *temper*. Sometimes, too, it requires so much exertion of thought,—is such a strain upon the mind,—that it hardly can answer the purposes of relaxation. If you play, by all means read Franklin's Essay on the Morals of Chess. For clearness of head, for truth-telling simplicity and honesty of purpose, and for perspicuity and liveliness of style, Franklin has, perhaps, no superior.

Always recollect that improvement, moral and intellectual, is the great object for which you were sent to Oxford. With that object nothing must be suffered to interfere.

I remain, &c. &c.

LETTER VIII
EXPENSES, AND RUNNING IN DEBT

MY DEAR NEPHEW,

I do not know exactly what allowance your father has been able to give you, but whatever it may be, I trust that you are resolutely determined to keep within it. This will, of course, require a good deal of care and attention. Many young men, when, upon going to the University, they find in their pockets a much larger sum than they ever possessed before, fancy themselves rich, and at liberty to allow themselves various unnecessary indulgences. The consequence is, that they become entangled in debts, from which they can never extricate themselves during their continuance at Oxford. Be on your guard against getting thus hampered. Take it for granted, that the regular and necessary claims upon your finances will leave but little over for the indulgence of pleasure or fancy.

The expenses of an University education are often most unfairly exaggerated by writers and speakers, who are fond of running down all old institutions. These carpers affect to set down to the score of the University all the money that is spent by the young men who reside in it. They seem to forget that, wherever a young man may be, he must eat and drink, and must purchase clothes suitable to his station in society. I was myself, as you probably know, at Christ Church, where I took my degree, and afterwards became a Fellow of Oriel. At Oriel, (which may probably be taken as a fair average of the rest of the University,) the *necessary* annual expenses of a commoner are from 70*l.* to 80*l.*, or thereabouts101:1 . This includes room-rent, batels, (that is, breakfast, dinner, &c. *exclusive* of tea and sugar), tuition, University and College dues, coals, letters, washing, servants. The University dues are less than 1*l.* per annum. There are, perhaps, few places in England, where a gentleman can be comfortably lodged and boarded at a much cheaper rate. Still there will always be many incidental expenses, and you must put in practice a pretty severe economy in order to meet them.

In the manner in which you spend your money, as in every thing else, accustom yourself to a certain degree of self-denial. Do not buy any thing merely because it hits your fancy, and you think you should *like to have it,* but consider whether you cannot easily *do without it*. Be as liberal as you can reasonably afford to be in assisting others, especially the poor, but spend as little as you can help upon yourself. Above all, never buy, or order, any thing which you are unable to pay for.

The habit of running in debt is pregnant with evil and misery of every description. It often—perhaps generally—amounts to positive dishonesty. The money which you owe a tradesman is really his property. The articles, which you have received from him, are hardly your own, until you have paid for them. If you keep them, without paying for them when the seller wishes and asks for payment, you deprive a man of that which belongs to him; and is not that something approaching to robbery? To a man possessed of proper feeling and a nice sense of honour, it must be very painful to suffer a tradesman to ask twice for what is clearly his right. To affect to be offended with such an application, and to meet it with superciliousness and insolence, is injustice carried to its height.

The manner in which some men, who would be ready to shoot any one who disputed their claims to be considered as gentlemen, treat their creditors, whom they choose to call *duns*, would, from its contrariety to any thing like reason, be almost ludicrous, if it were not so culpable, so cruel, and so dishonest.

A tradesman, from not being able to recover the money owed to him, sees himself in danger of losing his credit, and, together with his credit, the means of getting a maintenance; he sees his wife and children perhaps upon the very verge of misery, and yet, if he civilly asks for what is his due, he is considered as troublesome and impertinent, perhaps reproached and insulted!

Upon this subject I shall allow myself to quote the words of Delany, the friend of Dean Swift, one of the most animated and sensible of our sermon writers.

"Running in debt with tradesmen, and neglecting to pay them in due time, is utterly ruinous to the whole business of trade and commerce, and absolutely destructive of the very principles upon which it is built, and by which it subsists; and yet this is a crime every day committed by men of fortune and quality, with as little remorse as they eat and drink; and if the tradesman demands his money, it is odds but he is either threatened or turned into a jest. The son of Sirach's wise observation is here every day verified, merely substituting the words *rich* and *poor*, for the words *debtor* and *creditor*. *The debtor hath done wrong, and yet he threateneth; the creditor is wronged, and yet he must entreat also.* If threats will not rid these men of their importunate creditors, then are they to be deluded with fair words and plausible excuses, to pay attendance from day to day, to the loss of more time, and neglect of more business, than perhaps the debt is worth; and so the first injury, instead of being repaired is doubled. And yet the *gentleman* debtor, the author of this evil, is so far from repenting of it, that it is odds but he vaunts his wit and dexterity in doing it. *As a mad man* (saith Solomon) *who casteth firebrands, arrows, and death: so is the man that deceiveth his neighbour, and saith, Am I not in jest?* And, indeed, it is scarce to be conceived how any man can deal more destruction and ruin around him, than by deceiving and breaking faith with the fair trader; for it is well known, his credit, his whole subsistence, depends upon keeping his word, and being strictly punctual in his payments and his promises; and, if he fail in these, he is undone at once. And how is it possible he should not fail, if the gentlemen he deals with fail him? He hath no way of raising money but by sale of his goods; and if those to whom they are trusted will not pay him, it is impossible he can pay his creditors; and, if he do not pay them, it is impossible but he must be ruined, and, perhaps, many more with him. For traders are linked and dependent on one another; and one man's fall throws down many more with him: the shop-keeper is in debt to the maker or the merchant; and these again to the journeyman, the farmer, or the foreign correspondent; and so the ruin becomes complicated, and extended beyond imagination!"

"Credit is to a tradesman what honour is to a gentleman: to a man that is truly such, (a gentleman,) his honour is as dear as his life: to the trader, credit is as life itself; for he cannot live without it."

You, my dear nephew, will never, I trust, stoop so low as to be guilty of such dishonesty. But then you must keep a vigilant eye upon your expenses. Paying ready money for every thing may be sometimes inconvenient, and may, perhaps, occasion mistakes; but never leave Oxford for a vacation without clearing off every thing that you owe. Take receipts, and keep them. The most honest and respectable tradesman may sometimes, in the hurry of business, omit to cross a charge out of his book, and will feel a satisfaction in having any doubt as to payment removed. Have such receipts tied up and docketed, so that you may refer to any one of them readily.

Never suffer yourself to be led into needless expense by the example of your companions, and never be ashamed of saying that you cannot afford it.

We sometimes see weak young men vying with each other in the expensive elegance of their furniture and dress, or in the luxury of their entertainments. A man of large fortune produces at his table a variety of costly wines, abundance of ice, and a splendid dessert. Others, from a silly vanity, affect to do the same, although such expensive luxuries are altogether inconsistent with their finances, and with the general habits of men in their rank of life. The more such expenses and foolish ostentation can be checked by the college *authorities* the better. At all events, do not *you* be so weak as to fall into them. There is no disgrace in being poor, but there is disgrace and dishonesty too, in contracting debts which you are unable to discharge.

Some young Oxonians, I am afraid, after spending the larger portion of their allowance upon amusements and self-indulgence, drive off the payment of what they regard as their more *creditable* debts till they take their degree, under the idea that they will then be paid by their fathers. This is a most unwarrantable,—sometimes a *cruel*,—drain upon parental kindness. Poets may well speak of university expenses "pinching parents black and blue112:1 ," when this is the case.

The majority of parents, as I have already said, do not send their sons to the University without some degree of pecuniary inconvenience to themselves. It is, indeed, hard upon them, when, in addition to an annual allowance, which, probably, they have furnished not without difficulty, they are called upon for a considerable sum, in order to save their sons' credit—perhaps in order to enable him to take his degree. For you are aware that an unpaid tradesman has the power, if he thinks fit to exert it, of stopping the degree of a spendthrift under-graduate. This power, I believe, is seldom, if ever, exercised. But surely the being liable to it, through your own misconduct and extravagance, would be attended with a feeling of painful humiliation.

I remain,
My dear Nephew,
Your affectionate Uncle.

101:1 June, 1832.
112:1 Cowper.

LETTER IX
TEMPERANCE

My dear Nephew,

In the present state of society, it is, perhaps, less necessary than it would have been formerly, that I should give you any caution or advice on the subject of *temperance*. Five-and-thirty years ago, it was customary to drink a good deal of wine after dinner, and young men at Oxford were not behind-hand with the rest of the world in complying with this bad custom.

It was *then* generally the system, to initiate a freshman by making him completely drunk. Scripture is by no means sufficiently listened to *now*, but perhaps its warnings were less known and less regarded *then*. The master of the revels and his abettors were ignorant, or unmindful, of the threatenings denounced by the voice of Inspiration,—*Woe unto him that giveth his neighbour drink, that puttest thy bottle to him, and makest him drunken also:* and again—*Woe unto them that are mighty to drink wine, and men of strength to mingle strong drink.* Regardless of these denunciations, and trusting to the strength of their own heads, and the practised discipline of their own stomachs, their *noble* ambition was to make drunk as many of their guests as possible, especially any luckless freshman who chanced to be of the party. Those who, whether from religious principle or from manliness of character, did not choose to submit to be made drunk, were obliged either to encounter these *kind* endeavours with sturdy resistance,—resistance which sometimes occasioned a total cessation of intercourse and acquaintance,— or to evade them by stratagem. Glass after glass was dexterously emptied upon the carpet under the table, or the purple stream sought concealment under heaps of walnut-shells and orange-peel. In short, at a tolerably large wine-party there was wasted, or *worse than wasted*, a quantity of Port wine sufficient to check the ravages of a typhus fever in an entire village.

These days of *Celtic barbarism* are, I hope, utterly passed away. As in general society very little wine is consumed, (*excepting at dinner,*) so Oxford has caught the spirit of the times, and the bacchanalian revels to which I have alluded are, I believe, much less common than they were formerly, if not entirely exploded. I am afraid, however, that even now more wine is drunk in some colleges, than is consistent either with Christian temperance, or with habits of study, or with the preservation of health.

I need not point out to *you*, my dear nephew, the evils which, in a religious point of view, result from drinking to excess. You, I well know, would shudder at the idea of wilfully depriving yourself of reason, and of sinking yourself to the situation of a beast or of a maniac. A man, who has thrown away his reason, has little right to hope for the continuance of the assisting and preventing grace of God. And destitute of the controlling guidance, both of reason and of Divine Grace, what is there left to prevent his ungoverned passions from carrying him into the most perilous excesses? There are deadly vices, to which young men are, at all times, but too powerfully solicited by their natural appetites; and when those appetites are stimulated by drinking, and all salutary control shaken off, the danger is great indeed. You perhaps may remember an Eastern apologue to the following effect, (I know not where to find it): The Devil having, by the impulse of terror, induced a holy man to consent to commit *some* crime, allowed him to choose, whether he would get drunk, or be guilty of either of two of the most horrible enormities he could conceive. The poor victim chose drunkenness, as being the least offence, but in the state to which he had thus brought himself, was guilty of all three.

And even if you are kept back from any additional guilt, yet you well know, that by throwing away your reason, you become capable of being guilty of all sorts of absurdities,—that you are liable to say and do a hundred foolish things, of which, when you return to your senses, you will be heartily ashamed,—that you expose yourself to the ridicule and contempt of those, who witness the degraded state to which you have reduced yourself.

A drunken *Christian* is almost a contradiction in terms; and something the same may be said of a drunken *gentleman*. Among many in the middle and the industrious classes of society, there is much intelligence, much quick perception of what is morally right, and of general propriety of behaviour. As such men are not backward in shewing respect, where respect is really due, so they are keen-sighted in detecting gross inconsistencies of conduct, and ready to bestow the full measure of contempt upon those, who, while placed above them by the advantages of birth, and fortune, and education, yet meanly condescend, by their vices and their excesses, to degrade themselves below them.

The inconsistency of any excess in drinking, with the main purpose for which you were sent to Oxford, is palpable. You go to Oxford professedly for study. Independently of the time actually occupied by a wine-party, any excess will, probably, indispose you for study the morning after;

> Corpus onustum
> Hesternis vitiis animum quoque prægravat una,
> Atque affigit humo divinæ particulam auræ.

You will rise from your bed heavy and languid, probably with some disposition to headache; and will be far more inclined to lounge in an easy-chair, or to saunter about in listless idleness, than to sit down to active mental exertion.

I must add, that the habit of drinking much wine during your continuance at Oxford, is not unlikely materially to injure your health in the succeeding periods of your life. Such habit has a tendency permanently to derange and weaken the digestive powers, and to injure and harden the internal coats and the orifices of the stomach. I am persuaded, that much of the tendency to apoplectic and paralytic affections; much of the general indisposition, which we often witness in men advanced beyond the middle period of the usual term of human life,—men who have of late perhaps, lived temperately—is to be attributed to the wine which they drank when young.

But I will not dwell longer on the evils of excessive drinking. You know the admonitions of Scripture,—*Take heed lest at any time your hearts be overcharged with surfeiting and drunkenness. Be not drunk with wine, wherein is excess.* You know that *drunkards cannot inherit the kingdom of God*; you know that drunkenness is spoken of by St. Paul as being the vice of those, who remain sunk in the thick darkness of ignorance and heathenism, and as utterly unbefitting those who are blessed with the light of the Gospel. Indeed, it is unworthy of any man possessed only of common sense.

Guard, then, my dear nephew, against this degrading habit with determined resolution. Let neither the example, nor the solicitations, nor the taunting jests of your companions, induce you to demean yourself so far, as to be guilty of a vice so utterly unworthy of you, both as a man and as a Christian. If they, for their amusement, were to request you to cut off your right hand, you would not feel bound to comply with them. Do not, for their gratification, expose yourself in the condition of a fool, or an idiot. Do not, in order to please a party of thoughtless revellers, incur the displeasure of Almighty God, and run the hazard of eternal ruin.

And take care, that you do not yourself *acquire* a taste for any such sensual indulgences. "The appetite for intoxicating liquors," says Paley, "appears to be almost always *acquired*." Guard against the first beginnings of intemperance. *Principiis obsta.* If you are not on your guard, you will be in danger of being carried on, step by step, until retreat becomes out of the question.

You would avoid many trials of your firmness, and be relieved probably from much irksome importunity, if you could make up your mind to renounce wine altogether. This you would do with the less difficulty, if backed by the sanction of medical advice. I apprehend that most medical men, if desired to give their *candid* opinion, would recommend abstinence from wine as conducive to a *young* man's health both of body and mind. I knew *water-drinkers* at Oxford, who yielded to none of their companions in liveliness and all social qualities, either in their own room or at the wine-party of a friend. Many young men in the army, I believe, adopt this system, from motives both of moral and of economical prudence. A pint, or even half a pint, of wine per day, makes a considerable hole in the pay of a subaltern, or in the stipend of a country curate, or in the allowance of a briefless barrister. Avoid acquiring factitious wants. Do not by habit make wine necessary to your comfort. It is wise, when young, not to indulge in luxuries which in any future period of your life you probably will not be able to afford, consistently with the claims which will then be pressing upon you. I throw out this idea, however, for your own consideration, without urging it as matter of positive advice. I think, however, that your intellect will be clearer, and your mind often more cheerful, if you comply with the suggestion.

Shall I add a word or two upon temperance in *eating*? I hope that there are few young men who are apt to be guilty of the *porcine* vice of eating to excess; in plain English—of *gluttony*. Perhaps, however, the temptations of a well-appointed dinner, prepared by an exquisite *artiste*, may induce them occasionally to transgress. It is, perhaps, hardly fair to quote from any thing so well known as Addison's paper on Temperance, in the Spectator128:1 , but it is much to my purpose. "It is said of Diogenes, that meeting a young man who was going to a feast, he took him up in the street, and carried him home to his friends, as one who was running into imminent danger, had not he prevented him. What would that philosopher have said, had he been present at the luxury of a modern meal? Would he not have thought the master of a family mad, and have begged his servants to tie down his hands, had he seen him devour fowl, fish, and flesh; swallow oil and vinegar, wines and spices; throw down salads of twenty different sorts, sauces of a hundred ingredients, confections and fruits of numberless sweets and flavours? What unnatural motions and counter-ferments must such a medley of intemperance produce in the body? For my part, when I behold a fashionable table, set out in all its magnificence, I fancy that I see gouts and dropsies, fevers and lethargies, with innumerable distempers, lying in ambuscade among the dishes."

"Nature delights in the most plain and simple diet." He then gives some rules for temperance, which are well worth attending to. This passage of Addison is much in the spirit of that of Horace:

> — —"Variæ res
> Ut noceant homini, credas, memor illius escæ
> Quæ simplex olim tibi sederit. At simul assis
> Miscueris elixa, simul conchylia turdis;
> Dulcia se in bilem vertent, stomachoque tumultum
> Lenta feret pituita."

Most of the modern writers on dietetics, as well as those who have preceded them, recommend a very considerable abridgment of the quantity of food, usually consumed at the table of the affluent.

And while I strongly advise you to be rather abstemious as to *quantity* of food, so I wish you not to be in the slightest degree fastidious as to its *quality*, provided it is wholesome, and free from qualities absolutely revolting. You may naturally like one thing better than another, and partake of what you prefer, when it comes in your way; but it is painful to see a young man of any intellect indulging in the niceties of an epicure, and really appearing to care much about what he eats, and what he drinks. When I commenced the life of a country clergyman, I was often received, with almost parental kindness, in a house, in which good taste of all kinds,—moral, intellectual, social, and *culinary*,—presided in an eminent degree. Every now and then, some particular dish made its appearance, under the impression that I was particularly fond of it. Probably I had eaten of it some days before, because it chanced to be near me, or from some similar accident. I was grateful for the kindness and attention, but felt mortified, almost degraded, at its being supposed that I cared about one thing more than another, where all were good and wholesome.

Do not get into the habit of spending your money in ices, and other delicacies, at the pastry-cook's and confectioner's. You say that you are hungry;—

> "— — — —Panis
> Latrantem stomachum bene leniet."

If your hunger would disdain a piece of dry bread, it certainly has no claim to be attended to at all. You say that you can *afford* to indulge yourself in the delicacies to which I have alluded. I do not think that you can; at all events, your money may be more worthily spent—

"Non est melius quo insumere possis?
Cur eget indignus quisquam, te divite? Quare
Templa ruunt antiqua Deûm?"

In other words, if you have the money to spare, give it to the deserving poor, or to the Church-building Society. Few expenses are more unsatisfactory in retrospect,—I had almost said, more *disgraceful*,—than those which have been incurred by sensual self-indulgence; incurred to gratify a vitiated palate and a pampered appetite.

Self-denial is recommended by the classical writers of antiquity, as well as by the most sensible of modern authors; and, what is of infinitely more importance, is strongly inculcated by the Christian religion. But how shall self-denial be practised *at all*, if it cannot be practised in the low matter of eating and drinking?

Read again and again the paper of Addison, and the Satire of Horace, (the second of the second Book), from which I have made my quotations. Read also the following passages from that accurate observer of the habits and manners of social life, the son of Sirach:

If thou sit at a bountiful table, be not greedy upon it, and say not, There is much meat on it. — Eat, as it becometh a man, those things that are set before thee; and devour not, lest thou be hated. Leave off first for manners' sake; and be not insatiable, lest thou offend.

A very little is sufficient for a man well nurtured, and he fetcheth not his wind short upon his bed.

Sound sleep cometh of moderate eating; he riseth early, and his wits are with him: but the pain of watching, and choler, and pangs of the belly, are with an insatiable man.

I remain,
My dear Nephew,
Your affectionate Uncle.

128:1 No. 195.

LETTER X
ENGLISH READING

MY DEAR NEPHEW,

When at Oxford, you will not have much time for any reading, excepting that which has some reference to your examination. During the vacations, however, which occupy about half the year, you are more at liberty, and will do well, as I have already suggested to you, to give a good deal of your leisure to increasing your acquaintance with the classical writers of your own language.

Both at Oxford and home, endeavour, on most days, to catch some little portion of time,—a quarter of an hour may be sufficient,—for religious reading. Melmoth's "Great Importance of a Religious Life," and the abridgment of Law's "Serious Call," adopted by the Society for Promoting Christian Knowledge, are two of the best books that occur to me, for the purpose of impressing you with the absolute necessity, of giving religion the first place in your thoughts and your heart. You may read either of them through in an hour. Of the former, 42,000 copies were sold in the eighteen years preceding 1784. I mention this as an evidence of its popularity.

Some thirty years ago I was requested by a friend, to recommend some practical book to put into the hands of a young person. I named Nelson's "Practice of True Devotion," and have since seen no reason to alter my opinion. Let that be one of the first books that you make use of. If you read *one* chapter each day (and do not read more), it will last you about three weeks. After an interval of a year or so, go through it again.

Take next for this purpose Jeremy Taylor's "Holy Living and Dying," first reading (if you can borrow the book) what is said of this work by his highly-gifted and most amiable editor, Bishop Heber. One passage from Heber's remarks I must allow myself to quote: "But I will not select, where all may be read with advantage, and can hardly be read without admiration. To clothe virtue in its most picturesque and attractive colouring; to enforce with all the terrors of the divine law, its essential obligations; and to distinguish, in almost every instance most successfully, between what is prudent and what is necessary; what may fitly be done, and what cannot safely be left undone;—this is the triumph of a Christian moralist; and this Jeremy Taylor has, in a great degree, achieved in his Discourse on Holy Living." You will recollect that this book was written nearly two hundred years ago, and must not be surprised if you find a few expressions, and one or two sentiments, rather obsolete. One of the five rules which Taylor gives in his Dedication, "for the application of the counsels which follow," applies to all books of a similar character. "They that will, with profit, make use of the proper instruments of virtue, must so live as if they were always under the physician's hand. For the counsels of religion are not to be applied to the distempers of the soul, as men used to take hellebore; *but they must dwell together with the spirit of a man, and be twisted about his understanding for ever: they must be used like nourishment, that is, by a daily care and meditation*—not like a single medicine, and upon the actual pressure of a present necessity."

The genuine spirit of Jeremy Taylor, with more correctness of taste, is found in that delightful book, "The Christian Year." Read it repeatedly. It is every where full of poetry, and of the purest devotional feeling. The more you are imbued with the spirit which pervades that beautiful volume, the more fit you will be to have your part in "the communion of saints," among *the spirits of just men made perfect*.

Archbishop Seeker's Lectures on the Catechism, contain a body of divinity, doctrinal and practical, singularly judicious and useful. They are full of good sense and accurate information. The style, perhaps, is rather involved, and not very engaging; but you see a mind in full possession of its subject, anxious to put you in full possession of it also, without omitting any thing of importance.

Gilpin's Lectures on the Catechism are of a different character. This also is a very good and a very pleasing book, written with a particular view to young persons engaged in reading the Greek and Latin Classics.

Ogden's Sermons, on Prayer, the Creed, and the Ten Commandments, &c. are the offspring of a clear and powerful intellect, expressed in language remarkably perspicuous and elegant.

After these books, take some opportunity of reading the Sermons of Bishop Butler, including the Preface. This is not a book to be read in a room full of brothers and sisters. It demands close attention, and will give some exercise to all your intellectual powers; but it richly merits to have such attention and pains bestowed upon it. It deserves, indeed requires, more than a single reading. After Butler's Sermons read his "Analogy."

You will do well, at any odd intervals, or *snatches* of time, to make yourself familiar with Addison and Johnson. False delicacy shall not prevent me from recommending the selection from the writings of Addison which I made a few years ago. My reasons for making such selection are given in the Preface. The same reasons now induce me to recommend it to you.

Johnson requires no pruning. You can hardly read a paper in the Rambler or Idler, and, I will add, the Adventurer, without deriving from it some improvement, either moral or intellectual, or both. The structure and cadence of Johnson's sentences is certainly monotonous; but I seldom read half a page without being struck by the depth of his thought, the accuracy and minuteness of his observation, and the astonishing extent of his multifarious reading.

In order to enter with more discrimination into the style of our different authors, read often "Blair's Lectures." They are, I believe, sometimes spoken slightingly of by men of learning; I, however, as an unlearned man, think them particularly useful. The Lecture on the Origin of Language, indeed, the absurdity of which has been exposed with so much playfulness by Cowper, might well have been omitted.

I have already advised you, during the two longer vacations, to acquire, or to keep up, some knowledge of modern history. Russell's "Modern Europe" is, upon the whole, a useful book. It is, perhaps, too compendious; and I dislike its being given in the form of letters. Robertson's "Charles the Fifth" you have probably read already; if not, read it carefully when, in Russell, you arrive at the period at which it commences. Pay particular attention to the First Book. Perhaps Robertson was not sufficiently impressed with the importance and the effects of the Reformation in Germany; and he formed, I think, an unfair estimate of the character and motives of Luther. This matter will, I doubt not, be shortly set right in the Life of Luther about to be given to the public by one of the ablest and most learned men of the present day147:1 .

With respect to the history of our own country, I hardly know what advice to give you. Hume's style is very pleasing, but he cannot be implicitly depended on, especially where religion and the ministers of religion are concerned.

Henry's "History of Great Britain" is a very good and accurate book; but the continuity of the narrative is broken by the multiplicity of divisions in each period, (learning, arts, commerce, manners, &c. &c.), and by the transitions to the history of Scotland.

Lingard I have not read; I am told that his style is good, and his information extensive. It was natural that, as a zealous Romanist, he should seek to extenuate the faults of men of his own persuasion, and to exaggerate the failings, and place in an unfavourable point of view the motives and actions of the assailants of Popery; but he has, I think, been fully convicted of carrying misrepresentation beyond all reasonable bounds. There was but too much of bigotry and persecution on both sides.

Turner's History is, I believe, strictly honest and impartial, and a work of prodigious labour and research.

But in our attention to prose writers, we must not forget the classical poets of our own country. Make yourself familiarly acquainted with Shakspeare, Milton, and Pope. The more you read of Young and Cowper, the better. Young is sometimes turgid, with a good deal of bad taste; but he abounds in real poetry, and in strong truths most forcibly expressed. Cowper sometimes carries simplicity to the verge of being prosaic; but he is generally graceful, often pathetic, and sometimes approaches to sublimity. Of both, it was the common object to increase the influence of genuine Christianity; of both, the perusal has a direct tendency to make you a better and a more religious man.

Two of our most distinguished living poets—Sir Walter Scott and Southey—have seen their poetry cast into shade by the popularity of their own prose. The poems of both will live, and have justice done them by posterity. "Madoc" was many years ago recommended to me by one of the most able, and most candid, of our living authors. I read it with much interest. "The Curse of Kehama" is full of high and wild poetry; and "Roderick, the last of the Goths" gives a noble picture of deep penitence and of devoted patriotism. You will hardly read any ten lines of the longer poems of Sir Walter Scott, without meeting with some striking beauty of expression or of sentiment.

I am afraid, however, that the English poets, both those of former times and those of the present day, have been, in great measure, superseded, among you young Oxonians, by Lord Byron. In almost every under-graduate's room that I happen to enter, *he* seems to have taken possession. Lord Byron, as a poet, has certainly many transcendant merits,—merits which are peculiarly fascinating to young men. The interest which I,—which *every one*,—naturally must feel in the moral and intellectual habits and pursuits of such an important portion of the community, makes me deeply lament the noble poet's excessive popularity among you. I am perfectly aware, that by the following remarks I shall expose myself to the indignation of some men, and, possibly, to the contempt of others: but I feel that my opinion on this subject is not taken up on slight grounds; and I *must say my say.*

The publication of Lord Byron's life and correspondence has contributed, a good deal, to divest him of that mystery, which hung about him, and in which he himself so much delighted; and has brought him down rather more to the level of ordinary mortals. They show him to us as a man possessed of splendid talents, of extensive and various attainments, and of the *seeds* of many noble and generous qualities; but as a man actuated by ungovernable passions, and by an overweening opinion of his own superiority to all other mortals. *Self,* whether intellectual or sensual, seems to have been the idol that he worshipped. *His own* antient family, *his own* talents, *his own* attainments, *his own* whims, *his own* passions, *his own* excesses, seem all to have furnished food for his vanity, because they were *his own.*

I acknowledge that, in all the circumstances of his *bringing up*, he was singularly unfortunate. His early destitution, the character and habits of his mother, the neglect of his noble relations, the venal praises of his parasites and dependents, all acted upon his character with pernicious influence.

> "Untaught in youth his heart to tame,
> His springs of life were poison'd."

He was sensitively alive to all the beauties and the sublimities of external nature, and had a most penetrating insight into the complicated feelings, and the various workings of the human heart, with all its passions and affections; consequently, he abounds in passages of great beauty, and of singular strength and power. The gratification derived from the perusal of such passages, however, to a man at least who really believes himself to be an immortal and a responsible being, is but a poor compensation for the moral effects of many of his poems, his *later* poems more especially155:1 . They too often appear to breathe a spirit of engrossing selfishness; a spirit of captious and gloomy scepticism,—scepticism extending, not only to revelation, but to the primary truths of what is called natural religion, and even the most acknowledged bonds of moral obligation. The tendency of his writings is to make you dissatisfied with almost every thing, and every body in this world, and at the same time to unfit you for the world to come; indeed, to make you doubt, whether the idea of a world to come is not altogether a mere delusion.

Lord Byron particularly excels in describing female loveliness, and the effect which such loveliness produces upon the ardent temperament of youth. In fact, the feeling within themselves so much that responds to these descriptions, is one great cause of the popularity of Lord Byron among young people. The sensations to which I allude, however, are of themselves but too importunate. It is most unwise to excite them,—to give them additional energy,—by the perusal of the high-wrought and glowing descriptions of this poet of the passions.

I had heard much of Don Juan, and felt some curiosity to read it; but I was aware of the manner in which bold and flippant ribaldry sometimes takes hold of the mind, even when shocked at it. I knew well, that human nature has in itself but too much of passion and sensuality, without needing any additional stimulus. I was unwilling "to soil my mind" when I could avoid it. For my own sake, I was unwilling to see the most destructive vices treated as mere matter of jest, and the most awful truths of religion introduced in connexion with ludicrous images, and spoken of in the language of mockery. However much our judgment may disapprove of these things, yet the ludicrous passages and images are too apt to stick by us, even when we most wish to shake them off.

A book was advertised, called "The Beauties of Don Juan, including those passages only which are calculated to extend the real fame of Lord Byron." The editor acknowledges that the poem itself, from the unpruned luxuriance of the author's powers, "has remained a sealed volume"—certainly it *ought* to be a *sealed volume*—"to the fairest portion of the community." This *expurgate* selection, however, though it contains many passages of great beauty, is a book which I should be sorry indeed to place in the hands of any young lady; and one against which I would *forewarn* every young man, who is not prepared to run the risk of sacrificing, at the shrine of genius, Christian faith, and Christian soberness, and Christian purity.

The description of the shipwreck had been spoken of as particularly fine. I read it. Not long since several accounts of actual shipwrecks and disasters at sea were published159:1 . Some of these accounts, are among the most interesting and edifying narratives, that I am acquainted with. They abound in instances of heroic courage, of unshaken endurance, of a noble disregard of self, of the warmest benevolence, and of the most exalted piety. Don Juan seems to have taken a wayward pleasure in culling from these narratives the most distressing and painful facts, and then mixing them up in doggrel verse, with ludicrous images and ludicrous rhymes; the main *wit* often consisting in some unexpected absurdity of sound or cadence.

One of the most dreadful consequences of shipwreck is, when a remnant of the crew, cast off in an open boat, are reduced, by extremity of hunger, to determine by lot, which of them shall first be made the food of his companions. Even in such calamity, this perverse and bitter spirit contrives to find matter for merriment. He laughed in himself when he wrote the stanzas, and tries to make his readers laugh; though they must feel indignant with themselves if they give way to the impulse.

I conclude my letter with two sayings of Bishop Horne's. "He who sacrifices religion to wit, like the people mentioned by Ælian, worships a fly, and offers up an ox to it." Again; "Sir Peter Lely made it a rule, never to look at a bad picture, having found, by experience, that, whenever he did so, his pencil took a tint from it. Apply this to bad books and bad company."

However brilliant the talents of a writer may be, yet, if a book has a tendency to produce a bad effect upon the moral habits of the mind, that book is a *bad* book.

> "When I behold a genius bright and base,
> Of tow'ring talents, and terrestrial aims;
> Methinks I see, as thrown from her high sphere,
> The glorious fragments of a soul immortal,
> With rubbish mixt, and glitt'ring in the dust."

I remain,
My dear Nephew,
Your affectionate Uncle.

147:1 Rev. Hugh James Rose.

155:1 Childe Harold and the *four* first tales (I am speaking only of the larger works) are most free from objection, at the same time that they are the most beautiful and interesting.

159:1 The Loss of the Kent, and Narratives of the Shipwrecks of the Lady Hobart packet, the Cabalva, &c. &c.

PRAYERS

A Prayer before Study.

(FROM DR. JOHNSON.)

Almighty God, in whose hands are all the powers of man; who givest understanding and takest it away; who, as it seemeth good unto thee, enlightenest the thoughts of the simple, and darkenest the meditations of the wise, be present with me in my studies and inquiries.

Grant, O Lord, that I may not lavish away the life which thou hast given me on useless trifles, nor waste it in vain searches after things which thou hast hidden from me.

Enable me, by thy Holy Spirit, so to shun sloth and negligence, that every day may discharge part of the task which thou hast allotted me; and so further with thy help that labour which, without thy help, must be ineffectual, that I may obtain in all my undertakings such success as will most promote thy glory, and the salvation of my own soul, for the sake of Jesus Christ.

Prayer after Time unprofitably spent.

(FROM DR. JOHNSON.)

O Lord, in whose hands are life and death; by whose power I am sustained, and by whose mercy I am spared, look down upon me with pity. Forgive me, that I have this day neglected the duty which thou hast assigned to it, and suffered the hours, of which I must give account, to pass away without any endeavour to accomplish thy will, or to promote my own salvation. Make me to remember, O God, that every day is thy gift, and ought to be used according to thy command. Grant me, therefore, so to repent of my negligence, that I may obtain mercy from thee, and pass the time which thou shalt yet allow me in diligent performance of thy commands, through Jesus Christ. *Amen.*

Prayer for Temperance.

(FROM BISHOP JEREMY TAYLOR.)

O Almighty God and gracious Father of men and angels, who openest thy hand and fillest all things living with plenty; and hast provided for thy servant sufficient to satisfy all my needs: teach me to use thy creatures soberly and temperately, that I may not with loads of meat and drink make the temptations of my enemy to prevail upon me, or my spirit unapt for the performance of my duty, or my body healthless, or my affections sensual and unholy. O my God, never suffer that the blessings which thou givest me may minister either to sin or sickness, but to health, and holiness, and thanksgiving; that in the strength of thy provision I may cheerfully, and actively, and diligently serve thee; that I may worthily feast at thy table here, and be accounted worthy, through thy grace, to be admitted to thy table hereafter, through Jesus Christ, our Mediator and Redeemer. *Amen.*

Prayer for the right government of the tongue.

O God, watch over me this day for good; and grant that I may so keep the door of my mouth that I may not speak unadvisedly with my lips. Preserve me from offending with my tongue either against charity or purity. Let me not be guilty of foolish and immodest talking and jesting, of evil-speaking or censoriousness, or of any other of the many sins of the tongue. Grant that all my conversation may be such as becometh one who professes to be the servant and disciple of thy beloved Son, in whose name I beseech thee to hear my prayers.

www.ingramcontent.com/pod-product-compliance
Lightning Source LLC
LaVergne TN
LVHW041757190726
843493LV00008B/2661